Research in

The Role of a Researcher in Executive Search

By Hugo Stevens

Copyright © 2016 by Hugo Stevens

All rights reserved. No part of this publication may be reproduced, distributed, or transmitted in any form or by any means, including photocopying, recording, or other electronic or mechanical methods, without the prior written permission of the publisher, except in the case of brief quotations embodied in critical reviews and certain other noncommercial uses permitted by copyright law.

Contents

1. Pre-mandate research 9

Prioritisation 10

Background to the pitch 12

The prospect 13

The decision-makers 14

Background research 16

The role 18

A couple of calls 20

Pitch preparation notes 21

Rehearse 23

Pitch 24

You don't have all the answers 27

Proposal 28

Research strategy 29

2. Briefing/research discussion 31

Teaming up 31

Target organisations 34

Communication...36

A few other details about the strategy... 38

The candidate specification 39

3. The search...44

List of candidates 45

List of sources 47

Painstakingly thorough 49

Information management..52

Sourcing 53

Emailing sources 54

Calling sources 57

Sources' objections...58

Approaches 61

Approach call to candidates...63

Candidates' objections..65

Follow-up calls 66

Unconventional research tactics...68

Diary/time management...69

Mapping...70

Communication with client: progress update, longlist and shortlist 72

End of the research and...of this book..................................74

Introduction

This short guide aims to address the gap of information that is publicly available about the still obscure world of research in executive search. Even if the days of headhunters with black books would seem to be long gone at a time when the transparency of tools like LinkedIn is revolutionising the industry, the role of researcher has still received very little attention by market participants and outside observers alike. The purpose of this guide is simple. To gather in a clear and straight-forward manner the core activities a researcher can follow to succeed in that extremely important role they perform in executive search. It is intended for three main groups of people:

- Graduates or professionals in other industries that are considering taking a role as a researcher in an executive search firm.
- Researchers already working in executive search that wish to review the research methodology they follow and, perhaps, get a few new tips or ideas which they can implement in their jobs.
- Researchers from other industries who are intellectually curious to understand more about the role of a researcher in executive search, and learn practices which they could potentially adopt to their current fields of operation.

The text is based on many years of experience in the industry. It doesn't pretend to be exhaustive nor the definite best practice approach. It is, nevertheless, the result of a conscious effort to summarise and distill in short chapters the key and most relevant aspects of the research methodology in executive search, offering one of the few guides of its kind – if not the first one– to the market.

1. Pre-mandate research

Before a researcher starts doing the research to identify talent for any role, their headhunting firm needs to actually win a search mandate. If you are working as a researcher in an executive search firm, winning business will not be your main responsibility. It is the consultants who are responsible for managing relationships with clients and generating fees. However, depending on the size of the organisation and the structure of the team you are a part of, as a researcher you may be asked to help your team prepare for a pitch. This situation will take place when your organisation has been invited to discuss a specific search requirement at an institution (the prospect). For instance, if you are a headhunter in the consumer sector you may be invited to pitch for, let's say, a Sales Director (the role) at Best Grooming Products (i.e. the prospect). This invitation could be result of an existing relationship of your firm with Best Grooming Products because they are already an existing client, or simply because by reputation the prospect knows of your company and they view it as a potential search partner – as part of a panel of other search firms they are also talking to. This is really a beauty parade, where a number of search firms will compete to be the chosen one to carry out the search the prospect is looking to launch. The background of the invitation to pitch is quite important as that will have an influence in the type of preparation you need to do ahead of that crucial meeting.

Prioritisation

Another consideration you need to take into account is that, often, invitations to pitch are given at very short notice. So, as ever in the life of a headhunter, you need to learn to juggle a number of deadlines and prioritise work accordingly. In this sense, there is not golden rule as to what level of priority pitch preparation would have in your diary. The obvious thing to say is that any headhunting organisation, if it's going to survive, needs to win new business. Therefore, pitching for new business is often viewed as something critical that tends to take priority over existing searches. The counter-argument to that is that if your organisation prides itself of delivering best in class results, the execution of existing research projects, at the highest standard and on time, should also be a top priority. Still, many headhunting firms will prioritise resources to ensure they win new business and the delivery of existing projects becomes something that "needs to be managed" accordingly. It may even be that as a researcher you will receive pressure from one of your colleagues who demands you to deliver research results on a specific search assignment, whilst another of your colleagues needs your help to do preparation for a pitch.

 Unfortunately, you have limited resources and the amount of time you dedicate to each project will inevitably have an effect on the result of other projects you are also handling. This is one of the many conflicts that a researcher – often feeling quite lonely – will need to manage carefully. Ultimately, it will depend on how your responsibilities have been agreed with your line managers. In most cases, a researcher's primary responsibility will be to deliver existing work (longlists, mapping projects, etc.), and preparation for pitches will be something consultants should be accountable for.

Sometimes, however, your prioritisation will be affected by the type of career progression you wish to seek. Pitch experience, i.e. origination of new business, could open many doors for other roles in executive search, particularly the path to a fee-earning/consultant role. The other consideration to keep in mind is that pitch preparation is to a certain extent contingent work – you only get paid if you win the project. So it could be a waste of your time if your firm doesn't win the pitch. On the other hand, work on existing projects/searches is paid in advance (through retainers) or at least on delivery of results. Also, delivering work for existing clients is a way of doing business development – by keeping a happy client which could award your organisation other projects in future.

Once you know the priority you are giving to doing background research for the pitch and decided how much of your diary you allocate to it, you will need to understand a few points to make your work most efficient.

So we're only starting to learn about the role of researcher and you already realise how prioritisation will be a key part of the role of a researcher. There are a number of considerations you need to review in order to evaluate how much of your time – your most valuable commodity – to each project you work on. Whichever way you prioritise, make sure you involve your internal stakeholders and everyone else involved knows how much input they can expect from you, avoiding last minute nasty surprises. Internal stakeholder is a key aspect of your role, so make sure you constantly communicate with them.

Background to the pitch

Firstly, you need to get a good understanding about how the invite to pitch has come about as it will give you many clues about what sort of work you need to do ahead of the meeting. Usually, a consultant in your firm will have had at least a conversation with the prospect, and will know some of the background of the role, reasons for the hire, and how it fits within the organisational structure. At this stage, it is perfectly normal that the information you possess is still limited, as it will be at the pitch meeting when you will get the opportunity to learn more about the specific search the prospect wants to start. It is your responsibility to speak with the consultant to gather as much information about the project as you can. You and the consultant will need to agree on what sort of information you are looking to identify. Again, you will need to be very honest with the consultant about how much of your time you will be able to commit to prepare for the pitch.

The prospect

The research you will do ahead of the pitch will be very different if it is for an existing client, or if it is for an organisation your firm has never dealt with before. Preparation will also greatly differ if it is for a well-known organisation or for a rather unknown one.

If the pitch is for an existing client it will naturally be easier for you to do the necessary research – most of the times, at least! The first part of the research will be in-house, looking at previous projects previously done by your firm for this client. You will seek to get an overview of the track record of success (or failure), types of roles filled etc. You will be keen to understand what type of research has been useful previously with that client and what hasn't. It is also an opportunity for you to evaluate what this client has already seen in a pitch from your firm and whether it is moment to start innovating and showing them something they haven't seen from before.

In addition to personally looking at the documentation related to previous pitches, you should speak to some of your colleagues that have done projects for this client before. That insight about the client's culture, what they like to see in presentations, their communication style, etc. is extremely valuable. Even if you only get 5-10 minutes from your colleagues they will be all the worthwhile. You never know what you could learn; maybe that client doesn't like lengthy presentations, or the opposite they are the type of client that enjoys detail, many examples, etc.

The decision-makers

Another angle you need to explore is your firm's experience with the particular individuals that will be present at the pitch and that will make the decision as to who they award the search to. For instance, it may be that you are going to meet a CEO and a Human Resources Director (HRD). The CEO could be someone your firm has been working with already, but the HRD could be new to the organisation. You should still check internally if that HRD had been a previous client of your firm as well as checking the HRD's work history (online) to learn in which organisations he/she worked at before. It could well be that before joining Best Grooming Products (to follow our example) the HRD worked at Smart New Technologies. In which case you should speak to any of your colleagues in your company to see if any they has had any dealings with Smart New Technologies as that information could give you some clues about what the HRD is like.

You need to remember that the executive search world is rather incestuous, so some of the people present in the pitch could be known to your organisation as had previously been candidates themselves. Search for that information and check if any of the individuals that will be present at the pitch have been dealt with as candidates by your firm previously. It will help you understand and prepare for the scenario before you and/or your colleagues are in it. This is an angle you need to get used to in executive search. Even though search firms like labelling people as clients, prospects, candidates or sources, one same individual could have different labels depending on the context. For instance, Jane Smith uses your organisation to hire people for her team – she's a client. But a couple of years ago she was a candidate and found her job thanks to your firm – so she was a candidate. At the same time, your firm gets in touch with Jane regularly to get references on people she knows in the market place – so she's also a source! Your firm should keep record of each interaction with Jane in every scenario, which all together will offer you a well-rounded picture of Jane. Don't underestimate how much that information can help you to prepare for the meeting and show Jane that you have done your homework properly. In any event, always be cautious about how you use any information you find that can be confidential.

Background research

Next step is to do a quick news search on-line or in trade magazines to find any relevant news related to the prospect in the last 6-12 months. Depending on the size of the prospect you could find an overwhelming amount of news stories, or the total opposite. When selecting 3-5 news stories you need to be mindful of which would be most relevant to the search the prospect is looking to start. You are looking for stories that will help you understand "what's going on" in that organisation, and will help you show the prospect during the pitch discussion that you are fully up to date with the issues that affect their organisation. (Remember this game of headhunting is not only about what you know, but about what other people think you know!). Note down the links to the news stories you have chosen and draft a brief outline of the news in your pitch-preparation sheet.

If the prospect is a listed company you will need to have a look at their annual reports, which they publish for their shareholders. These documents tend to be quite detailed and full of data. As an executive search researcher, no-one is expecting you to go through the detail of annual reports. Rather, you just need to get an overview of the organisation's financial performance, challenges, and opportunities. This is often well summarised in the first few pages of the report, so it shouldn't take more than just a few minutes to capture the key data contained in the report. Analysts' reports which may also be found on the clients' website are sometimes helpful too. Again, if what you are doing is executive search, you shouldn't get stuck on the minutia of this type of reports, which are primarily intended for investors. You are not an accountant, or an asset manager and you are not going to the pitch meeting to advice the prospect on how to improve their loss-ratio or earnings-per-share. However, that financial information could well be part of the basis of the discussion from which to link with the client's talent needs. That research could set you apart from other recruiters that haven't looked at that angle properly.

The role

Once you have gained a good understanding of the prospect, you need to look into the specifics of the role you have been invited to pitch for. Sometimes, you will be provided very limited information – due to confidentiality reasons or others. In other occasions, the consultant who had the initial pre-pitch discussion with the prospect will have been told a fair amount about the background of the role. If you are very lucky, you may even be sent a job specification in advance of the pitch.

You need to understand if the role is new to the organisation or it is a replacement. If someone has already been doing that same role in the prospect organisation you should get familiar with the background of that particular individual. This doesn't mean that the prospect will be looking for someone of the same background. However, knowledge of the incumbent's profile will make you be more prepared for the discussion. The reasons for replacing the incumbent could be many. It may be that they are moving on to another role (within the same organisation or elsewhere); it could be that they are retiring, being made redundant etc. This is very valuable information to get prior to any pitch as it would have a major influence on how the pitch is structured; it will help you anticipate some questions the prospect may have for you and your team.

If your firm has done similar searches recently – in our example a Sales Director search for a major consumer goods company – you should get familiar with the issues encountered and market trends identified when doing those searches. Again, get five minutes from those of your colleagues that may have done those similar searches and ask the relevant questions: *"dear colleague, what can you tell me about that search in the consumer sector you did six months ago?"*

In the event that your firm hasn't got a recent track record in doing similar searches, you should go externally to find what you need to know about the role. Initially do a quick Internet search to understand what trends are affecting that specific role (as you will have already done with the industry). Particularly for senior roles like CEOs, CFOs, Head of Audits, etc. reports published by the Big Four (KPMG, PWC, EY, Deloitte) are very useful; as they also are publications by the strategy consulting firms like BCG, McKinsey etc. Again, you won't have time to read everything that's out there. Find the most recent information which should be easily identified by their title and focus your attention on the executive summaries which outline the contents of those reports. Only if you feel the strong need to get further understanding of a specific point, you should go to the report itself.

A couple of calls

It is not time to start calling the market about this search yet. However, when doing background research for a new project, you should reach out to two or three participants in the market, i.e. people that are doing similar roles in competitors or organisations of similar nature of the prospect.

You can approach them on a "general basis". Basically, you will call, let's say, the Sales Director of X consumer good company and perhaps the number 2 of Y consumer company. You will speak to them to get an understanding of their experience, career motivations, and their views on the market they operate. The information you gather in these introductory calls could place advantageously when you meet the prospect at the pitch – it would make them feel you are in touch with the market and aware of current trends. Who knows, if you win the pitch you may be able to get back to those individuals you had had the introductory call with and now you can discuss a specific role with them. One of them could even end up getting the job!

In most cases, when you have these general introductory calls you should not mention the identity of your prospect. You can just simply say you are calling them because you are in the market and expect hiring activity in that specific sector in the coming months. You could be even more specific and say you expect to win a related search assignment in the coming weeks. However, under no circumstance you should get into guessing names about who the prospect may be. It is advisable to leave it very generic and just say you are active in the sector hence the interest to connect with them.

Pitch preparation notes

Now is the moment to get together with the rest of the project team and start sharing notes. It's expected that the project leader (consultant) should have a view on how they are going to structure the pitch. Your job is to ensure that in two or three pages you have captured all the relevant information you have been gathering in previous days. That intelligence can then be used to choose which themes will be the priorities in your presentation, hoping that they will resonate with the client and make them press the "buy" bottom.

Depending on the internal resources of your organisation, you may be asked to put the presentation together (usually in PowerPoint), although that could be done by a specialist in presentations in PowerPoint (or whatever format). This topic is beyond the scope of this book, but as a general rule if you are responsible for creating the presentation a few of the key points the prospect would like to see are:

- Your firm understands the issues, challenges, and opportunities of their prospect and their sector.
- Your firm's understanding of the role and skills required.
- Key themes to discuss in the meeting (confidentiality, reason for hiring, internal candidates, expectations about the role, etc.).
- Your firm's track record of success with the prospect; or in similar roles at other relevant organisations.
- You firm's differentiators as a search partner, and its benefits for clients.
- Profiles of potential candidates you feel could be relevant (anonymised).
- Search process: structure, communication timelines, documentation.
- T&Cs of business, I.e. fees.

- Team biographies, so they prospect can see you and your colleagues are fully qualified search professionals to undertake the project.

Rehearse

If you are attending the pitch, it is worth spending a few minutes with the consultants and agree who in the team will speak about specific topics during the pitch meeting (always communicating and agreeing everything with your team!)The expectation is that consultants will lead on the pitch and will do majority of the selling. However, it is also important that as a researcher you say play your part in it as you will be performing a crucial role in the team that will deliver the project. Often, it is the moment to explain the research process or when talking about relevant market participants (who you may have spoken to in recent days) that would be most ideal for you to participate. If you help yourself with video recording devices to hear how you come across even better!

Pitch

So you have had maybe just a couple of days to do all the preparation prior to the pitch and now it's the moment when the prospect decides if they award your firm the search or if all your work in previous days has been wasted. Again, as a researcher you should not be accountable for the success of the pitch, though you clearly have a vested interest to make it succeed.

As described in the previous chapter, it will be the consultants that will direct on how the pitch should go and your role should be in supporting them and following their lead. However, there will be occasions when the pitch doesn't go "according to plan" and no matter how much preparation and rehearsal you have done you will still need to improvise.

If you have never been in a pitch situation, imagine a room where there are one, two, three people or even more that work for the prospect organisation. Depending on the type of hire, this could well be the Board (or some members of it) Executives, and more often than not the HR Director or Head of Human Resources.

It may be required that you introduce yourself (even if you think you don't need to, it is not a bad idea you rehearse this introduction prior the meeting). Remember that people make judgments based on their initial impressions of someone, so it is imperative you sound confident, explain clearly and succinctly what you would be doing in the project, and ideally show some previous and recent relevant experience in similar searches.

If you are going to explain the research process you follow when doing a search you should also have ideally rehearsed it previously. Though most firms' research processes are very similar, the devil is always in the detail – how thorough and systematic, or creative and flexible you are about doing that research. So expect some members of the panel to ask you questions about your market knowledge, sourcing strategy, previous experience in similar searches, etc. This guide covers the basics you need to know about the process, but it is up to you to follow rigorously the process and therefore be confident and come across credible when explaining it to the client.

If you are going to talk about profiles of people that could be relevant candidates for the search, you need to be mindful of confidentiality issues. Best advice is to keep anonymous any profiles of concept candidates you will speak about, avoiding mentioning their names or even the organisations they work for. For instance, if you are discussing a Sales Director role, you can show your knowledge of the market by saying something like "we know Sales Directors at similar organisations that are on a total compensation of c. $500,000 ". But you shouldn't say "Eliana Pissola, Sales Director at Fun Toys Company makes $500,000" Confidentiality and discretion are a must in a good headhunter.

Similarly, when talking about the market more generally,unless your sources tell you otherwise, you should not disclose their identity either. For instance instead of saying "Mike Rogers, CEO of X company told me about this issue and what a big headache is for him to find good Sales Directors with international experience", you should keep it anonymous and say something like "in one of my recent conversation with the CEO of a well-known firm in the sector it was highlighted the high priority this is for him to have international experience in his senior sales force" . Your credibility will go up several notches and you will not jeopardise your sources.

Something you also need to bear in mind is that if your firm wins the project you will be responsible for doing much of the delivery and you will face many unknowns during your research. Consultants, sometimes– though not always – are more eager to win a project than to understand some of the details or logistics that the research for it will entail. So it is up to you to ask any relevant questions you feel are critical to get a good understanding of the role that will help you deliver it successfully. A note of caution though, you should not get stuck in minutia that is not relevant at this stage. In other words, if you raise an issue or a question it should be relevant and important and you should follow up with some sort of feedback about how you would take that particular issue into account in the way you would do research. For instance, if the prospect responds to one of your questions saying that international experience is crucial for the candidates, you should make a comment on its relevance for the search. For instance, saying *"candidates with international experience are in high demand and they are usually given great flexibility to work remotely"*. Any valuable information you can provide the prospect at this stage about the considerations for the search will be very useful for them– and they will really appreciate your input.

It is common that once you win the pitch there will be opportunity for further briefings with the prospect (which becomes a client), where you can ask more detailed questions about the search you have just won. So the most relevant questions in the pitch are the ones that have a fundamental bearing on your proposal of a research strategy.

You don't have all the answers

Don't pretend you have all the answers at this stage. What you bring to the pitch meeting is your intellectual ability to understand issues, to ask the right questions and to show you can follow thoroughly the right research process to find answers to those questions. Remember, clients will be paying you to go out to the market and find something they want, rather than paying you for something you already have. This is a fine distinction difficult to understand for some researchers, who think they should know all the answers. You will be familiar and understand issues of the market having done previous background research, but given the unique peculiarities of each search assignment, there should always be unknowns you need to investigate further. You need to be comfortable with "not knowing all the answers". If you struggle to accept this, just take a few minutes to read again the previous lines and think about it, interiorise it. Once you are comfortable with that idea, your confidence in yourself and your research process will increase substantially.

Proposal

Following the pitch, it is often common that the search firm will revert within a day or two with a proposal of business, outlining their understanding of the opportunity, proposing a strategy for the search, and also including the commercial terms and conditions of business. By all accounts the bulk of this task should be responsibility of the consultant, and it is outside the scope of this book. However, you may be required to help with notes, ideas, and most certainly with the research strategy. You and the project team that attended the pitch will have a meeting to agree on the key issues/considerations of the search, and their influence on the research strategy. This is the time you can show you understand the issues of the search, you know what questions are being asked, and you propose the avenues to find solutions for your client.

Research strategy

So from a researcher's perspective your key contribution when putting the proposal will relate to the research strategy. Given your understanding of the role and your knowledge of the market you will tell the prospect, succinctly and clearly, how you would go about doing the research to ensure you find the right candidates. What sort of institutions you would target I.e. key competitors, etc. Would you look for candidates outside the sector your client operates? If so, what sectors would you look at and why? Some people would also include a target list of institutions where you are intending to poach people from. You could even add a few profiles of individuals you know and you are intending to approach (again, anonymised to keep candidates' confidentiality). As you will have noticed, much of this work was already done in the background research prior to the pitch meeting. The difference is that, after having had the benefit of learning more about the role in the pitch, you are now able to further refine your research strategy and tweak if necessary.

Some search firms like to include the candidate specification as part of the proposal. This could be a good idea if you already have all the details you think you would need to carry out that search. As previously said, sometimes, search firms will have a briefing discussion with the client after they have won the pitch so they can get into the nitty gritty of the role and produce the candidate specification from there. So it depends on how your firm works, but if your employer's common practice is to include a candidate specification as part of the proposal, this will be your responsibility. We will cover the elaboration of the candidate specification in a dedicated chapter later on.

In summary, in most firms your responsibility in the proposal will be concentrated on the research strategy, maybe including names of target institutions, anonymized profiles, even updated track record or case study (an overview of a similar or relevant search your firm completed successfully in the past); in some cases, also writing the candidate specification. You can use visuals to make your research process easier to understand. Make sure the client knows what to expect from you, particularly in relation to timelines, methods of communication, and documentation they will receive from you.

2. Briefing/research discussion

Well done, your team has won the mandate and you now have a search to work on. All the efforts for preparing the pitch and the thoughts put in the proposal have paid off!

Teaming up

It is now time for you to sit down with your project team (consultants, assistants, and maybe other researchers) to agree on strategy, deliverables, allocate work, and discuss timelines and everything else. Much of this work has already been done. You have already thought of the research avenues where you are going to be identifying candidates. More likely than not, you have also thought of which candidates you may know, or which sources you can call that may be able to help you find candidates. What you do now is to ensure all your internal stakeholders – the project team – are on the same page regarding the research strategy to follow and what is expected of everyone, so there aren't surprises at a later day. This is not an easy task, so make sure everything is very clear about the plan that's been agreed, and keep an audit trail by putting it in writing!

Depending on the level of seniority or type of search, the consultant may want to be involved in the sourcing and approaching of candidates. Let's assume this is a very senior role, the consultant will probably want to call many of their key contacts to tell them about this high-profile appointment your firm is handling so their contacts know your firm is a key player in the search business. (Naturally, consultants will call their contacts with the excuse of getting advice and recommendations, which is clearly a priority too, rather than calling to specifically say how great they are for having won this search).

Consultants will also want to call key people in the industry even if they don't know them yet. This search offers them the perfect excuse to pick up the phone and call the CEO of that organisation they have been aiming to speak to for quite some time. The call will naturally be along the lines of *"we are doing this search, are you able to recommend anyone that could be a good candidate..."*. But the underlying idea is that this call is a business development opportunity for your firm. On the back of that call, that CEO may be impressed or intrigued about your firm and keen to know more about your services in a follow up meeting. Although your take on these calls won't be exactly as with the consultants, you may also see the opportunity to open the door to a potential client and arrange for your team to go and meet with a particular organisation. That's added value!

Sometimes, the timeframes are so tight that the research phase of the mandate cannot just be relied on one researcher and it's all hands on deck to ensure your firm will deliver the results expected on time. When there are many people working on the assignment, it is imperative that you and your team are clear on the calling list. If you can't do that in this initial briefing meeting (maybe because you still need to do the identification of names for your calling list) there will be another follow up meeting within a few days where the various calls will be clearly allocated to the different team members. You should always register in writing, which sourcing or approaches calls each member of the project team is responsible for.

Remember, the whole aim of setting up this research strategy meeting is to agree on a plan which the whole project team thinks is the best to achieve the best possible results for your client within the agreed timeline. You do that by clearly allocating individual responsibilities and expectations, and regular updates/communication with your project colleagues to ensure everything is going according to plan. Keep up the internal communication!

Target organisations

It is time to agree and list the target organisations where you are going to headhunt people from. Depending on the type of search you will have to do, it could be a very straightforward job – though never easy. It will be about listing key competitors and identifying people that hold relevant positions in those organisations. Relevant positions would be either those with the same job title as the one your client is seeking to fill, or perhaps some roles whose natural next step up would be the job your client is looking to appoint. The obvious caveat to bear in mind here is the size of organisation. Candidates in smaller organisations could be interested in a job with a title of lower ranking in much bigger organisations. Other consideration is that sometimes people that are in organisations going through a period of trouble will also consider "lower level" roles as they don't see a great future in their current employer. Those considerations should be part of your strategy and have an effect on the target list.

In other occasions your search will be much broader than targeting the "usual suspects" in competitors' or organisations of similar nature to your client's. This gives you an opportunity to be creative and to look in places that may not be obvious but that could well offer the right solutions to your clients. You will need to agree with the consultant – and ideally have spoken to your client – about the broader research options you want to explore. For instance, if you are working for an insurance firm, the obvious competitors would be other insurance firms. However, you could also find valid candidates in adjacent sectors, such as retail banking, credit cards companies or even further afield, like professional services, telecoms or utilities companies. You need to be very clear from the start that your client would consider such options. And even if your client is a bit reluctant of these options but you feel very strong about their viability you should challenge your clients' thinking and offer some out of the box ideas for them. Naturally, you must be able to explain why those candidates from outside your client's core sector would be relevant to your client's organisation. Remember that you only have limited amount of time to carry out the research (whilst you are also doing other projects) so you must understand well what are the top priorities (which institutions, sectors, and candidates) and what search avenues are lower priorities.

Communication

The timeframes and regularity of communication will have been agreed in the pitch or proposal, but it is crucial that everyone in your team is aware of them and you have your own internal deadlines prior to the client deadlines. You will discuss this in the research briefing meeting. In any case, you (or the team's assistant) will ensure those deadlines are visible in the calendars of each member of this project team. You should agree how often you will touch base with your colleagues. Ideally will be more than once a week, though that will clearly depend on the profile of this project and how often you are communicating with your client.

Clients will often want to have a weekly report or update call to understand what progress is being made. It is in your benefit to ensure those calls/updates are in the diary as you want to start getting the client's feedback on progress of the search as soon as possible. Imagine you wait to get their feedback until the end of your research, and then you learn that the findings you are producing are not what your client expected! There is also an element of taking your client along with you on your research journey, so, they understand the context of the candidates you find, and their decision is an ongoing process rather than a snap reaction during a longlist or shortlist meeting.

This communication should be backed up by documentation showing the progress being made. In most cases, the research documentation will be your responsibility – certainly with regards to content, though formatting could well be done by the team assistant. If you are going to have support from an assistant, ensure they know what their input is going to be and when they will need to keep space free in their diaries to help you out with the documents, whether it's with formatting, doing data input, or anything else. It should be very clear from start what documents are going to be sent out to the client, what they should look like and which input is needed from each member of the team. You will most likely want the members of the project team to review the document before it's sent out to the client.

A few other details about the strategy...

A note of caution regarding the research strategy –it is not uncommon that after one or two weeks of research and as a result of the increase of your understanding of the specific market, you will broaden the search into other areas that you hadn't thought of before. You could also rule out some research avenues which, after a few calls, became apparent weren't right to find suitable candidates. It is OK. No-one expects you to know all the answers right at the beginning of the search. It is a learning process. What's important is that you put the right volume of calls, talk to the right people, and ask the right questions. Modifying slightly your search is a step closer to your goal – not away from it.

As part of this discussion, it may be obvious that you will need to ask advice from some of your colleagues whose input could be very valuable. Amongst your team, you will also specify who is talking to whom within your firm to get that advice internally. Don't underestimate this source of information. You are only going to get to your goal by asking help and sometimes the most helping hands could be sitting just a few meters away from your desk rather than in big seats of large corporations.

Another aspect which you should be very clear on at this stage is the confidentiality of the search. You need to understand if it is OK for you to disclose your client's identity when going to the market; or if otherwise, you need to keep their name confidential. Same with compensation details – is it OK to disclose or is it confidential or subject to candidate's experience?

By the time you and your team leave this meeting you should have a very clear picture of what lies ahead in the next few weeks, both in terms of what everyone is doing and how the team is communicating on a regular basis.

The candidate specification

So you have agreed a research plan, and it's now time to start putting it into action. The first task is to create the candidate specification. This is the document you are going to share with the market in order to identify and attract the right candidates. This is effectively a sales document so in no way it should resemble those dry, often meaningless, job specifications written by HR administrators. It should be a document that is attractive to read and that outlines the role in positive terms, whilst it also sets clearly defined criteria of the ideal candidate. The idea is that when "Mr or Ms right candidate" reads the specification, he or she goes "wow, this document was written for me, it's me who they are after and I would love to do that job!"

More broadly, these documents are a great marketing tool for your client to put their name in the market whether it's to talk about their great strategy of growth for the next phase of development, to reassure the market the company is taking measures to change course of action if they happen to be in difficult circumstances, or whatever else it could be relevant to their PR.

Remember, you will be your client's representative in the market for a few weeks and it's paramount you understand their message and are passionate about it. You should not be surprised by the fact that some people you will speak to during your research will want to learn not only about the specifics of this role you are searching for, but more broadly about the future plans of your client. In these conversations, you will also gather very valuable information about your client which you didn't know before. If you feel some of that information could have negative implications for the search (reputational issues etc.), you need to speak to your project team and potentially to the client about it.

In summary the candidate specification serves for:

- Attracting the right candidates.
- Making clear the key selection criteria for the role.
- Sending a broader message about your client to the market.

It usually consists of somewhere between four to ten pages, though it could be longer. Main points to be included in the candidate specification are:

- Cover page. So it's clear what the document it's about.
- Summary
- Introduction. This is optional but it is an opportunity for a senior member in your client's organisation, for instance the Chairman, to include a personal message thanking candidates for their interest in the opportunity and highlighting the importance of this role. It is often signed to add a personal touch.
- Background about the client. Including some of their history, their core activities and services, but also more current information such as relevant recent developments, financial information etc.
- The role. This is arguably the most important part of the document. It is here that candidates will see their excitement confirmed (or not) after a prior discussion they will have had with you. It should include information related to the background for the appointment, i.e. why this position is available. This matters as it helps candidates understand the context of the role within the organisation and its timing. It is also an exercise of transparency and of good PR. So if the reason for the hire is a counter-measure to some recent negative development in your client's business, by being transparent about it (when possible) it gives candidates the reassurance that the client is aware of their troubled position and are taking the right steps to tackle their problem. Think about it, if people in the market know your client has had, let's say, regulatory issues and those issues are not

addressed in the candidate specification (and in your message to the market) your client loses an opportunity to build trust in the marketplace – particularly with some people that could have been potential candidates.

- The description of the responsibilities should be composed in an engaging and attractive way. So rather than saying *"the role holder will have full accountability for ensuring XYZ so the company meets its strategic targets"*, which would pose the risk of sounding too prescriptive, you should focus on the benefits this role will bring to the appointed candidate. For instance you could say *"Responsible for the team that will deliver XYZ, you will have the opportunity to shape the future of this organisation and the market it operates"*. See the difference?

- About the ideal candidate. Similar to the previous point, it's about describing positively the skills needed for this role. You have the option of writing something like: *"You will have ten years of experience as CEO in the consumer market and a thorough understanding of the issues affecting the sector which will help the company achieve its strategic targets"* (that is the old-fashioned way of writing job specifications). Alternatively, you could say something along the lines of: *"already a proven CEO in their field, you will have strategic vision to grasp the current opportunities in the consumer market and lead our company to further success"*. Can you see the difference? A note of caution though. Even if you want to make the reading of this document engaging and exciting, you will need to avoid coming across as "fluffy" and abusing of adjectives like "extraordinary", "sensational" and the like. Limit its use, and stick to a factual style. So in those selected occasions that you use strong qualitative adjectives, they will be particularly powerful.

- Web links of interest. Usually to specific pages of the organisation's website (annual accounts, awards, etc.) or third party's websites that are relevant to the client (news stories, etc.).

- Biographies of key people involved in this selection process. It is useful for potential candidates to learn about the backgrounds of the client's key decision makers. In some markets, it is likely many candidates will have heard or might even know some of those people.
- Contact details. Just like any other document you will ever produce, your contact details should be visible so interested parties can contact you to discuss further.
- Organisational charts. This is to give candidates an understanding on how they would fit in within the organisation of the company.
- Location. Depending on the location of the role, it may be needed to add further information of interest about the particular city, state or country the job is located. Not to be overlooked, as sometimes the location of the role will prove to be the toughest sale to candidates.
- Visa, work permit requirements to be eligible for this appointment.
- Equality, diversity policy, etc. Your client's HR Department will be particularly keen to add their own text here.
- Application process including what's needed to apply for the position (CV, covering letter, other documents etc.) as well as the deadline to receive applications.

Traditionally, candidate specifications have been very wordy and have lacked images and pictures. Where possible you should include some images as long as they are relevant. The easiest way is to get them from the website or official documents from the client. Depending on the resources of your firm, you may work with a designer to make this document more visual and attractive.

Not all candidate specifications will have all these sections outlined above. However, this list hopefully helps you understand what a good candidate specification should look like. The result of a good candidate specification is that you will not only impress your candidates and sources, but also your client and even your colleagues!

3. The search

You have agreed the research strategy with your team, you have drafted the candidate specification and sent it to your client for their approval so you can then share it with the market.

Depending on your involvement in preparation for the pitch you may at this stage still need to do some background research on the client or the sector to understand trends, drivers etc. However, more often than not all that research would have been produced prior to the pitch so you already have a generic understanding of the market you are about the enter.

It is therefore now time to start the search! You will start populating the two main lists of contacts you will have for this assignment. One list will include sources, i e people you are going to call to ask for their advice for this search and get references on candidates. The other is the list of candidates. Ideally you will have a database that will allow you to have those two different lists under the same assignment. As discussed, at this stage you will already had produced a list previously, for the target organisations, which will rarely change much during the research – it will mainly be used as a reference tool.

List of candidates

As part of the research already done you will already have some names of potential candidates that you or your team knows. There will also be other profiles you don't know personally, but you have found them on your internal database or they are quite visible in the market – given what you have found out about their experience so far you think they could be potential candidates. You can start adding those names to the list of candidates.

Whenever you add a name to the system, you will need to clearly make a record that warns other people in your organization not to get in touch with this contact as you are calling imminently for your project. This helps internal communication within your firm and avoids embarrassing situations where two people at your firm will call the same person too close after each other, which could be perceived as unprofessional.

You start going through your target organisations, identifying people that could be good candidates. So at XYZ organisation John Smith and Mark Jones seem to be the most likely candidates, given their current titles. You will of course need to verify that that information is up to date. You can do this online, either using a number of databases such as regulatory listings, company websites or others, or you can quite simply call the switchboard of the organisation and asked for the exact title of Mr. Jones to be confirmed. If you think this is going to raise suspicions you can say you are intending to send some documentation but you want to ensure you have their details correct. If the operator does not want to validate the information you can always speak to the relevant assistant which more often than not will confirm their bosses' details for you.

Ideally, you will have started to populate the list of candidates with quite a few names; though still with a fair of number of "gaps" i.e. key seats in organisations you still don't know the incumbents' identity. Sourcing will help you filling those gaps.

List of sources

Just like you did with candidates, you will also need to add contacts to the list of sources you or your colleagues are intending to reach out to. Remember these are people that at this stage you don't feel they are candidates but rather sources of information for you. i.e. they will either recommend people they know that could be candidates or give you useful information for your research, which will confirm or add new angles to your research strategy.

These sources will be people you know, who may have been helpful in the past. So you now want to ask for their help again. Many other sources however, will be people you don't know, but given their profile in the industry you feel they are well-connected and able to make good recommendations of candidates.

A source could be someone that has direct experience of the sector in which your client operates —let's say in technology. Sometimes, you will find sources in areas adjacent to your client's. For instance, companies that serve this technology sector such as lawyers, bankers, or even journalists that know the area and can give you very good information about individuals working at technology firms. More specifically, you will be seeking to speak to people that have just left those target organisations in which you want to find candidates. These are often the best sources as they are willing to tell you all about their ex-employer, their team structure and everything you need to know at this stage about the best potential candidates you will find in a specific organisation.

A good way to identify those sources is in the section "people moves" of trade magazines (which usually offer a free trial). Also, the websites or the organisations you are targeting may have a media page where they refer to changes at the senior level with recent appointments and departures.

Other natural places are online databases, which sometimes offer the option to search people by previous organisations they worked at. So you if you know Jane Sullivan left ABC company three months ago, where she was a senior executive and she's now at JXY you can call her and ask her about her ex-colleagues: *"Jane, what did you think of Xi Chang that you worked with at ABC"*. Sometimes, Jane may even be able to offer an introduction to some of Xi if she feels the search you are carrying out could be a good opportunity for her (this obviously depends on the contractual restrictions she may still be obliged for a certain period of time after leaving her ex-employer).

You should do extensive internet search on relevant conferences that are related to the sector or role you are looking to fill. In most cases, you should have access to speakers's names. You should get in touch with them to ask for advice as they are bound to be extremely well-connected and offer you great advice and insight on specific individuals. More rarely, you may even have access to the whole list of attendees of that conference. This is less and less common, but look out for it as it could be a gold mine for you.

Painstakingly thorough

As part of your desk research you need to be very familiar with how Boolean searches work and depending on how niche is the area or market you are trying to cover you may need to research on internet search tools every single relevant name you identify. This is not doing a simple internet search most people do. This is about being painstakingly thorough. It may be tedious, but it there is any information out there you need to find it.

For instance, let's say you are doing a search in a very niche field in which you don't have any previous experience. It is for a senior management role of an accountancy firm specialist in the sports sector. Your client's competitors are not easy to identify. You may find some individuals working in large accountancy firms which will be visible. However, there may many other firms only known in the sports sector, which may keep a very low profile and not visible to those outside their professional circle. These firms will not come up just doing a regular internet search. For this reason you need to search every single new bit of information you obtain as your research progresses – whether it's the name of a new candidate or a new target company. You will be surprised what you can find. One of those searches may take you to a list of accountancy firms in the sports sector compiled somewhere, or it may take you to the list of attendees of a conference of the sector too. Depending on the popularity and number of results, you will logically need to narrow down the search.

For instance, let's say one of your sources recommends you to speak to Mario Suares, Senior Manager at sports accountancy firm Accounting Stars. You will obviously need to ensure that you get all the relevant information of current or previous employees in Accounting Stars' website. Do the same on LinkedIn or similar websites, and don't underestimate the power of search engines. Type "Mario Soares" on Google and see what comes up. If you get too many entries put "Mario Soares" and "accounting" or "accountancy" and it will narrow it down. Then, you can try "Mario Soares" and "sports". You could find an entry about a previous firm he worked at. That could be a new firm you didn't know about, and surprise, surprise they also do accounting for sports professionals. Another target organisation for you! Or maybe you see Mario's name in an article of a specialist magazines you didn't know about. You search the magazine for other articles and you find rich information for your search. Maybe you notice he was at a conference you hadn't heard of before. You check the conference panel, and next to Mario's name you find about a dozen of other contacts from other firms which are also competitors of your client and relevant target organisations for you. Keep doing this thorough internet search for any new names you find.

Success is about exploring every available avenue, opening a door at a time, noting down on your notepad what have you searched for and what haven't and keep logging the information on your system. It is the persistence and thoroughness of that detective work that will lead you to success. It is not glamorous, but very effective as many of your competitors will only do this partially. If you do a thorough job, you will not only be able to get a very accurate picture of the current structure of an organisation (which should always be confirmed later in conversations with the market) , but much of its history and changes preceding the current situation. Your list of names and companies will literally start sprawling and by the time you finish this part of the research your list of sources and candidates will be rich in individuals and companies you didn't know or hadn't thought about when the research started. All this before you even picked up the phone. You are already starting to connect the dots and form a view of the "whole picture" or "the candidate universe" i.e. what this specific market looks like and its key players. You can brief (and hopefully impress) your client about your findings in your next update call.

You may find that some of those names that are emerging were already in your database perhaps from a few years back, and maybe that's why they weren't visible when you first looked internally. You should understand which of your colleagues may have spoken to them. If they are still a warm contact it may be time to ask a fellow colleague to make a call on your behalf to reconnect with that particular individual. On occasions, going for a coffee with someone that already has a warm relationship with your firm could give everything you are after. That warm contact person could be happy to provide you with a list of contacts, phone numbers, references on potential candidates, sources, and in a half an hour coffee save you weeks of work. Try that option if you see it available!

Information management

As you have seen in previous chapters it is important that you record, and share with your colleagues the relevant information you gather as part of your research. It could be something basic like names of companies, sources, candidates but also other type of valuable intelligence which you will be able to share with your client. This gathering of trends in the industry, news, moves etc. will give you credibility when starting conversations with people as they will see you not only know about your client and the position but you seem to be fairly conversant about what's going on in their industry. After only a few days of doing research you are starting to realise how your knowledge about your client's field is significantly increasing.

You should have a system where that information is easily stored, accessed, and retrieved to input onto the documents you will send to your client. The more efficient this is done, the more it will help you in future searches. Most search firms will have very clear and strict guidelines about where and how you need to store that information. You don't need over-sophisticated systems to do it. Sometimes the most basic excel spreadsheet, with its different columns, filters etc. is a rather efficient way to manage that information. In the current day and age though, it is expected that your search firm will have a bespoke search database which will make your life much easier.

It is important is that you and the rest your team know the rules you are following to manage that information consistently. It's up to everyone to do it, though you as a researcher, will probably be adding your information and also monitoring what your team colleagues do (or don't) and chase for any potential missing information.

Sourcing

All right, so you now have the candidate specification approved by your client, and you have produced a list of potential sources (and possibly started the list of candidates too). It's time to get on the phone and start calling people. This is one of the activities that researchers, particularly inexperienced ones, tend to struggle more. The fear of calling someone senior they don't know, to talk about something that have limited knowledge of, and ask them quite sensitive questions about ex-colleagues or other people is, unsurprisingly, nerve-wrecking for some junior researchers.

If you follow all the right steps until now as explained in previous chapters you can surely succeed at sourcing. The most natural thing would be to start calling those sources that you have spoken to before, or at least someone at your firm has, so the call is warm and easier. In fact if it is a source you know well you can be honest with them and tell them you have just started this search of which you know very little about and need help. If you ask politely and appropriately your warm contacts will be delighted to help you.

In any case, whether a warm or cold source you should bear something in mind. People will help you because they expect you can also help them at some point in the future. From their perspective, you are a useful contact for them that could keep them informed about future opportunities that could interest them directly.

Emailing sources

It is advisable to initially email sources to arrange a conversation at a mutually convenient time. There are a number of benefits for this:

- You have the conversation when it's convenient to your source so you don't catch them in a bad moment and are, therefore, more likely to help you.
- You give time to your source to think about the search you are doing, and they may have sometime to start thinking about recommendations or any other piece of advice for you.
- You save a lot of time calling someone once avoiding the potentially long chain of voicemails and missed calls to each other. Remember those people you are about to speak to are very busy and so are you, at least for the next few weeks!

Some researchers tend to write a standard email, which they mailshot to all the sources that are hoping to speak to. Obviously, sources don't know that same email is being sent to probably 50 or 100 other people. This is a smart way to use technology and save a great deal of time. You craft one email and with the help of your system you sent one single email that reaches all the contacts. Obviously, prior to that, you will need to have obtained the right email address for those contacts. Something which more often than not, is quite easy to guess as companies tend to follow same email address format. For instance ABC company will usually follow name.surname@abccompany.com. XYZ company follows the format nsurname@xyz.com etc. Out of 100 your hit rate will probably be at least 90%. With the few ones when your email "bounces back" you will need to individually try to get their email by calling their office, or use other methods like LinkedIn.

Depending on how many sources you are trying to reach out and also depending on your style of work, you may send individual emails to each source. This method will be very time-consuming. However, let's bear in mind there are some people will only respond to emails if they feel it's been addressed to them personally. It's up to you which method you follow, just be aware of your time management and the likelihood of response using one or the other.

Whichever method you use, most of the text of the email will be the same for everyone. The difference is that if you send a personalised email you try to make reference to the name of the previous company the sources used to work for or why you think they can help you. In general the email, whether standard or personalised, should consist of three main points:

- Introduction. A greeting (addressing the contact by their name); an explanation of who you are and what you do. For instance:

  Dear Pierre, I am emailing you from the Technology Practice of YYY, the search firm.

- The reason you are getting in touch. For instance:

I am getting in touch to ask for your advice regarding a CFO search we are doing for ABC Company (If you can't reveal the name of the company you will need to describe it without giving it away). *They are one of the fastest-growing technology firms in the country. The ideal candidate will have:*

-Finance experience in a multinational

-In-depth knowledge of the technology sector

-Fluent in French, English, and Spanish

- Course of action.

  I appreciate the time pressure in your diary, but I wonder if given your experience in the sectors at firms like ZYZ, Best Technologies and Great Software, you may be able to point me out in the right direction and perhaps recommend someone that would meet the criteria.

Please let me know a convenient time for you and the best number to reach you on and I will give you a brief call.

The emails should not be too long, just give enough information so the recipient knows who you are, what you want and what action they need to take.

Also, remember you are going to send dozens of these emails for each search assignment; you will work on a number of searches at a time. If you don't ask sources to book a time in advance you could be getting a lot of callbacks a matter of days and be in embarrassing situations as you may not remember which search you contacted that person about. Most efficient is to agree a time in advance and put it in your diary.

Calling sources

So you have now agreed a time via email and you have the source's telephone number. Put it in your diary and make sure you set a reminder 10 -15 minutes before the call. When you get the reminder you should use those 10 minutes to refresh your memory with the background of the source (remember you have identified and contacted so many people that you are not expected to remember all of them!). Remember why you chose to get in touch and what exactly you want from them. Do you just want recommendations for the search, or are you thinking of referencing specific individuals you have already identified?

It's time to call them. Introduce yourself and ask them if it is still a convenient time for them to speak. If you haven't spoken before you should give them a very brief overview of your firm and yourself (brief, they will want to know something about you but not your whole career history). Keep it relevant to them. Refer back to your email, give them a bit more of background, reinforce why you chose to contact them and ask the relevant questions. *"Can you recommend anyone?" "Why do you recommend that specific person?" "Who was doing this job at your previous institutions?" "You have been in this market for a while, is there any advice you feel I should bear in mind whilst networking in this market?"*. As always, makes sure note down every information they give you as you will need to share it with your client.

Sources' objections

The sources may ask you questions. First one will be *"how did you get to me?"* It's time for you to be complimentary about their high profile in the industry. Again, if you haven't done so, it's time to remind them why you are getting in touch. You shouldn't spend much time on this part of the call. Just give them a bit of reassurance (if they need it) that you are a search professional; you know what you are doing; and why you are calling them specifically.

They may then start asking questions about the brief. Is your client looking for X or Y or Z skills? Be concise and clear. When you feel something is not too relevant, let them know that your client wasn't that specific about that particular aspect or skill. Always keep focus of the key criteria to identify relevant candidates. Those criteria should be clearly specified and visible in the candidate specification, and they drive much of your questioning and research. Don't get lost in long explanations. If they ask you something they feel it's very important to know and you don't know they answer, be honest. Say *"that question hasn't come up before, I may need to check this with my client and get back to you"*. If they can't think of any candidates, help them visualise what the ideal candidate should look like. Until now, you may have described the candidate according to specific criteria/experience/ skills. For instance: *"we are looking for candidates with 10 years of experience as CEO, and a strong finance background."* Now, it may be time to start putting some adjectives of the expected attributes of the candidates: *"the ideal candidate will be an experienced CEO that's very ambitious, a visionary, politically astute and good with numbers!"* Those attributes may help your source think of specific people.

A typical question that sources tend to ask is related to salary. Sources will ask this for a variety of reasons from pure curiosity to really understand which of their contacts may be open to looking at this from a financial point of view. How you answer this question will depend on whether your client has given you the liberty to disclose salary information to the market. If you can't disclose it, you will need to tell your sources that at this stage you don't have that information and are looking to get an unbiased understanding of the market including salary benchmark of relevant candidates.

They may be able to help and give you names or tell you to look into specific companies. Other times, they will want to think about it or ask you for more information so you can send them the candidate specification, and they can think of recommendations for you.

Some sources, they will just not be able to help. Always finish the call knowing if you need to follow up with them in any way and always appreciate their time. You don't know when you are going to need them next. If they have helped you tell them you hope to return the favor at some point or ask them directly if there's anything you can do for them. This is about receiving but also about giving. That's how it works.

Remember that the purpose of these sourcing calls is not about finding out who's looking for a job. As a researcher in executive search you are looking for the best talent. This is often people who are not actively looking to change jobs. Therefore, your line of questioning should be more about skills, attributes, experience, rather than *people that may be looking for a change"*.

Even if they can't give you any recommendations tell them, "*if in the next couple of weeks you come across anyone you think could be a good fit for this search, I would be delighted to hear from you"*. You will be surprised how many people will get back to you after days or weeks just because they had lunch or bumped into someone they hadn't originally thought of and now they realise that person could be a good candidate for your search.

Make sure you understand if the information the source gives you is confidential or if they are happy for you to tell the recommended candidate who recommended them. In fact, sometimes your sources may want to contact the recommended candidate themselves first and make the introduction to you. If the source wants to remain anonymous, keep your word and don't tell the recommended candidate about the source of the recommendation.

Make sure you record all the information they've given you, and if they have provided names of particular candidates do thorough desk research on them as described above. Does your company know them? If so ask colleagues that may have spoken to that candidate in the past. Put their name on Google or other search engines to find more background about them. Check them on online databases, companies websites etc. All that information you are getting should be validating your initial research strategy or it should be telling you that it is advisable you alter some of that strategy. If sources tell you something that you feel will dramatically change your understanding of the research strategy for the search, you should speak with the project team straight away and re-evaluate your plan.

Approaches

You have probably made a good deal of sourcing calls and you have started to get recommendations of candidates you now need to approach. Depending on how your firm structures its research process you may wait to approach potential candidates after the so-called "longlist" meeting or you may start as early as week one of your research. The earlier you start talking to candidates the earlier you start understanding how interesting the opportunity is for them, and also how good are those candidates you have been identifying. The benefit of waiting to the longlist to make the approaches is that you will be able to prioritise approaches of those candidates that look best (on paper at least) or even get guidance from your client in terms of which profiles they view as priority.

Whichever timing you chose to make the approaches the message to the candidates won't differ much. The key to making the approach call, just like everything else, is about preparation. As you did with the sources, it will help you if you set the call in advance, via email, to ensure the candidate you are looking to speak is actually available when you call them. The initial email, just like with the one you use for sources, could be a standard template email that you will send to all the candidates. Alternatively, you could write tailored emails to each candidate you are approaching. The email will consist of three key points:

- Introduction. Same as with the sources' email.
- Reason for getting in touch.
- Course of action

Below, an example of an approach email:

Dear Samir

I am emailing you from best consulting group, the executive search firm specialising in the industrials sector.

I am getting in touch with you as you have been highly recommended for a Chief Engineer Officer search we are carrying out for one of the top industrial groups of the country.

I wouldn't want to make assumption this is the right opportunity or timing for you, but I wonder if you may have a few spare moments for a brief discussion about it.

Please let me know your phone number and a convenient time for you and I will give you a quick call.

Looking forward to hearing from you.

Kind regards

The key to these emails is to make your message clear and succinct about your reason for getting in touch. Sometimes you may need to give a bit more detail than in the example above. So something like:

I am getting in touch as you have been recommended for Chief Engineering Search we are currently doing. My source described you as someone that has depth of experience in a leading engineering role with particular strengths in managing huge complex situations, which is the type of expertise my client is keen to attract.

This message should be enough to trigger interest of the prospective candidate. A few people may come back asking for the specification or salary details. Whether you do that or not it will depend on what has been agreed with the project team in the research strategy meeting. As a general rule, you should always aim to have a phone discussion with the candidate first, before releasing specification or indeed discussing compensation.

Approach call to candidates

So you have arranged a time with the potential candidate and are about to have the first call with them. Thankfully, you will have put this call in your diary and a reminder will have warned you 10-15 minutes in advance. Use that time to get familiar with the candidate's background (as you did with sources) and try to anticipate what questions you may have for them. As a rule of thumb, you should always know what exactly you are aiming to get from each call.

In this initial call, your goal is to finish the conversation with an interest from the candidate so they want to review the candidate specification. You also want to get a generic understanding of their suitability for the role. This initial call is not to go in great detail into the candidates' experience. It is a 10-15 minute call which starts developing your relationship with the candidate. Hopefully, at the end of the call you will have agreed to send them the candidate specification, and they will email you their CV in return. It is normal that the candidate will take a few days to review the specification and reflect about it. You should then have a follow-up call when you can answer any questions they may have about the opportunity, and you can also ask them any questions about their experience after reviewing their CV.

When you speak with the candidate ask them if this is still a convenient time and briefly introduce yourself and your company. You can then proceed to tell them about the search you are doing. Again, don't overload them with information. Be factual, succinct, and clear. Use pauses, let the candidate take everything in. Seek confirmation that they are following your story. Once you have finished your sales pitch, ask them for their feedback. If the volume of candidate calls is high or this candidate is not perceived as a top priority, you may prefer probing their interest with a close question, seeking a yes or no answer after you described the opportunity to them. Something like: "*would this opportunity be of interest to you?"* If you feel you may need to do a bit more work on the candidate's motivation, you will use open questions "how does this opportunity sound?" Or, *"how would this role fit with your current career plans?",* so they client has to give you more elaborate answers, which you can probe further.

Once you have sparked some interest in the candidate, it is then time to learn more about them. You will initially ask generic questions like: *"could you give me a brief overview about your current responsibilities?"* You can then start probing more on their experience in relation to the selection criteria of the candidate specification. For instance: *"how much international experience do you have to date?"*

Candidates' objections

Your aim, at this stage, is to keep doors open as long as you feel they could be relevant candidates for your search. Candidates will come up with a number of objections. Below, you will see a list (not comprehensive) of common objections presented by candidates and how you can overcome them.

- The candidate is "not looking for a new job". Candidates will often say that they appreciate the approach; the opportunity is great but they are not looking. The easiest way to respond to this is saying that opportunities such as this are rare and none can know when such an opportunity will knock at their door again. You can also emphasize that people you place are rarely actively looking to change roles, but they are opportunistic.
- Compensation. If you have given them a range of compensation and the candidate feels that's not attractive enough, you should warn them that this is still very early stages in the process and the client is also learning about the market value of good candidates. Sometimes clients do indeed increase the salary they were intending to initially pay for this role, after they realise they what the best candidates in the market are getting paid.
- The location of the role doesn't work for the candidate. Sometimes you will not be able to do anything about it. But sometimes it's possible to find a common solution as your client may consider letting someone work from home, at least a few days a week. Again, if you think it's reasonable, keep the door open and ask your client if they will consider the option for this appointment to work from home (assuming you don't have this information yet).
- Confidentiality concerns. Candidates don't want to be perceived in the market as "looking for a new job" and they sometimes may

Unconventional research tactics

We have gone through about how you should do research, getting information internally, doing desk research, asking your contacts in the market for recommendations and guidance etc. Some researchers would occasionally use other methods, more unconventional, whereby they call companies pretending to be someone else in order to get the names of people that are in those positions that will make them target candidates for your search. We won't go into the detail of this tactics neither we advise to follow this method. Just be aware that some of your competitors would do that.

Diary/time management

It could be argued this is one of the most important tools for success you will have as a researcher. Your projects will always have very strict deadlines and you will need to manage several projects at once. You are only going to manage a great delivery of your work if you have very strong time management skills. Your best ally will be your diary.

Pretty much everything that you do, whether you are doing desk research for a particular area, making sourcing calls, emailing candidates, producing documents for your client, preparing for the pitch and whatever else you can think of, should be in your diary. Whenever you look at your day or your week you should easily see your deadlines, what are you going to be doing each day, and potentially what spare time you may have. This is also helpful when you look back at a particular assignment and you try to quantify the time you spent doing it.

Use the diary, use the reminders, invite your project team to important events such as deadlines, team meetings. Be in control of your time and you will be in control of your searches. If helpful, you can use color coding to categorise events – say red colour for candidate calls, grey for desk research etc. Sometimes you will be forced to reorganise your diary and reschedule calls etc. depending on circumstances. One thing you will never want to reschedule it's the deadline to deliver work for clients. That's the most important event in your diary during the research process. Treat it as sacrosanct.

Mapping

In this guide, we have considered research mainly from the perspective of a search. This section refers to those projects when you will be asked to do a mapping project. You will not be searching for a specific role, but producing a document that outlines in detail a well-defined market segment, identifying every individual working at target organisations by their level and title. The skills and methodology needed for a mapping project don't differ from those already explained when doing a search. Think that whenever you do a search you need to map out a market anyway. One of the key differences is that you when doing the mapping will need to talk to people on a general basis but without telling them about a specific role your client is looking to fill. Your research and sourcing skills are still the same.

When mapping out a market you will call people and sometimes you will say you are doing background research as your client may be looking to hire in coming months, but you are not at liberty of confirming further details at this stage. In most cases, these mapping projects are very confidential and you cannot say anything at all about your client.

One of the big differences between a search and a mapping is the presentation of organisational charts, which is something your client will expect when you are delivering a mapping project. Sometimes your contacts in the market, insiders in organisations, will share with you their own internal organisational charts. Other times, you will have to produce them. This will be achieved by extensive sourcing, by talking to people in the team you are trying to map out and asking about their reports, their peers. You will validate all that information getting a coffee to one or two people and showing them they information you have so they can verify it. You will be surprised how open people are to tell you what the organisation really looks like and tell you are great, or you got a lot of that wrong!

Communication with client: progress update, longlist and shortlist

Commonly, search firms communicate with clients in a number of pre-defined stages including progress updates, longlists and shortlist. Remember that for all the research you produce you will need to produce reports that outline your findings. This is one of your key responsibilities, and should allocate time accordingly. Regarding the format of the reports will vary from firm to firm; more likely your firm will have clearly defined guidelines you need to follow. What's important is that if you have followed the research process systematically thus far, you should have all the relevant information and writing the report should be a fairly straight-forward job.

A progress update is usually held on a weekly basis. You would send your client a report in advance that shows the findings of your research so far. This usually relates to candidates identified, market trends arising, and any other market feedback of interest to the client, such as compensation levels of people you have been talking to, initial receptiveness to the opportunity, perception of the client in the market place etc. It is important you held these calls at least weekly so your client goes along with you in your search journey. They will provide feedback about those profiles you are presenting, and you will also start managing your client's expectations about what the market has to offer for that role your client is seeking to fill. At this stage, you will usually have limited information about the candidates so you will have to explain to your client that this is "work in progress" and you will gather more intelligence about the market and potential candidates as the search progresses.

A longlist is basically the list of all the candidates you are considering for this role. These are candidates that have been recommended to you, or you have identified as part of your research. Some of them you may have spoken to about the role; some others maybe you still haven't. The idea is that you go to your client with that list of profiles and you agree with the client which ones you are going to try to interview. Much of that discussion will be handled by the consultants, though you as researcher will be in the best position to influence – your consultant or your client – which candidates should be met as you have been speaking to many of them or hearing about them from the market. There is not an ideal number of candidates in a longlist. It could be 10, it could be 30 or 50. It really is quite open and dependent on the specifics of the search and the market you are operating.

A shortlist will be list of candidates "shorter" than the longlist and will include those candidates that have already been met by the consultant (maybe supported by you). It is the time your firm and the client agree on which candidates the client will meet directly. In this interview and shortlist stage your involvement as a researcher starts be secondary and it is then that the consultant starts taking the lead on the search, and you shift your focus to other new searches that may be coming up.

End of the research and...of this book

Following the shortlist, your client will interview candidates and they will eventually one of them will be appointed. But at this stage you have already done your job, you have identified the best possible talent for the role your client is looking to fill. Now it is up to your client to decide who they offer the job to. Little they know all the hard work, the innumerable conversations, analysis, chasing of sources and candidates, writing of reports you have had to do. But if you have followed the right process, you will have succeeded, so well done!

Hopefully this has been an enjoyable read and it helps you understand the research process to ensure you discover the best candidates in an executive search process. If you are considering a job as a researcher in executive search, this text may have helped you to decide whether this sort of career could be for you (or not) and hopefully perform well in some of the job interviews you will be having! If you are already working in executive search, it has hopefully been a good refresher and maybe has offered one or two new ideas for you to try as part of your research. Maybe you come from further afield and you are a researcher working in other industry outside executive search; may this read have brought some value to you too. To all of you, thanks for your reading and good luck with your research!

Printed in Great Britain
by Amazon